PENSIONS

Andrew Scrimshaw, a graduate of the University of Durham, is an Associate of the Pensions Management Institute. He has had over 14 years' experience in pensions consultancy, researching and advising on legal, regulatory and political developments affecting UK pensions. He has served on a number of pensions industry committees over the years and is a regular contributor to both trade and popular press. His publications include authorship of the CIPD's executive briefing, *Stakeholder Pensions* (CIPD, 2000).

CW01496311

The Chartered Institute of Personnel and Development is the leading publisher of books and reports for personnel and training professionals, students, and all those concerned with the effective management and development of people at work. For details of all our titles, please contact the Publishing Department:

tel 020-8263 3387

fax 020-8263 3850

e-mail publish@cipd.co.uk

The catalogue of all CIPD titles can be viewed on the CIPD website:

www.cipd.co.uk/publications

PENSIONS

ANDREW SCRIMSHAW

CHARTERED INSTITUTE OF PERSONNEL AND DEVELOPMENT

First published 2001

Design and typesetting by
Wyvern 21, Bristol

Printed in Great Britain by the Short Run Press, Exeter

British Library Cataloguing-in-Publication Data
A catalogue record for this book is available
from the British Library

ISBN 0-85292-929-3

Chartered Institute of Personnel and Development, CIPD House,
Camp Road, London SW19 4UX
Tel: 020-8971 9000 Fax: 020-8263 3333
E-mail: cipd@cipd.co.uk
Website: www.cipd.co.uk
Incorporated by Royal Charter. Registered charity no. 1079797.

Contents

Why should we offer a pension scheme?

> ☑ Introduction
> ☑ Motivational
> ☑ Competitive
> ☑ Financial
> ☑ Legislative
> ☑ Declining state benefits

Introduction

For the very large number of employees who are able to join a pension scheme, membership may be somewhat taken for granted. If questioned, few, if any, would deny that being in a pension scheme is advantageous, yet the scope and value of the benefits may not be fully understood.

Whilst pension schemes are complicated, difficult to communicate, costly to administer and seen by many finance directors as a drain on resources, most employers nonetheless instinctively feel that they ought to have one, even if they have not yet managed to get round to providing it. Despite the availability of other savings vehicles, pensions remain a key part of the remuneration strategy of vast numbers of employers.

Pensions are particularly dogged by jargon. Whilst this book seeks to avoid the worst excesses, a few key concepts are worth establishing at this early stage. At the most basic level, there are two predominant types of scheme: 'final salary' and 'money purchase'. Final salary schemes, which are typically provided by larger, traditional organisations, provide a pension linked to the employee's length of service and salary at retirement. In money purchase schemes, the employee and employer both pay contributions, typically a percentage of salary, into the individual's personal account within the scheme. This then grows with investment returns until retirement, at which point the resultant fund is used to purchase a pension.

Regardless of the name or structure of the scheme, the underlying idea is the same: to provide an income in retirement. The detail and merits of the different types of scheme are dealt with in later chapters, but the factors that influence employers' decisions to offer pension schemes may be broken down into the following:

- motivational
- competitive
- financial
- legislative
- declining state benefits.

Motivational

Over the last 10 or 15 years, the general public has become more knowledgeable about pension schemes and sees pensions as part of the overall remuneration package. In a world in which skilled, flexible and articulate employees are hard to recruit, pensions are seen as a key component of the benefit package. The level of benefit provided by the scheme will be considered in the same breath as working hours, holidays, share option plans and so on.

Employees clearly see pensions as part of their reward package, and pensions are used as a tool by employers to retain valued staff.

Competitive

In areas where employees have portable skills and job mobility is high, employers need to offer a pensions package that is competitive in the marketplace. As pension provision has developed, companies have begun to realise that one size does not fit all. A new high-tech company will require a different pension solution from a traditional old-economy manufacturer's.

Financial

Pension schemes are highly tax-efficient for both employees and employers, with companies obtaining corporation tax relief and employees obtaining income tax relief at their highest marginal rate on their contributions to schemes.

Equally, employer contributions to tax-approved schemes are not treated as a benefit in kind to the employee, and the employer does not have to pay National Insurance contributions on payments to pension schemes in the same way as it would do if the money was paid as salary (further detail is given in Chapter 2).

Legislative

The introduction of the Government's much-heralded stakeholder pensions will legally require employers, as a minimum, to provide employees with access to a pension scheme. It is open to speculation whether in due course some degree of compulsion actually to contribute will be introduced. Details of the stakeholder access requirements are given in Chapter 7.

Declining state benefits

The state pension will decline steadily as a proportion of national average earnings over the coming decades. This is largely due to such legislative changes as the 1981 change to the way the basic state pension is uprated (from linked to earnings to linked to price inflation). (However, lower earners will benefit from changes being made to the earnings-related second tier of the state pension system.)

Clearly, as less reliance can be placed on the state, greater pressure is placed upon employers to make provision for their employees. This is a clear intention of government policy.

What types of scheme exist?

☑ Funded or unfunded
☑ Final salary or money purchase
    Final salary (defined benefit)
    Money purchase (defined contribution)
☑ Occupational scheme or personal pension arrangement
☑ Tax-approved or unapproved
    Tax-approved schemes
    Unapproved schemes
☑ Contracting out
    Contracted-out salary-related (COSR) schemes
    Contracted-out money purchase (COMP) schemes
    Contracted-out ('appropriate') personal pensions
    Scheme design issues
☑ Stakeholder pensions

Having decided to offer the benefit of pension provision, a number of fundamental choices are open to the employer.

Funded or unfunded

Almost all mainstream private-sector pension arrangements operate on a 'funded' basis whereby assets are built up in a vehicle that is separate from the sponsoring employer. The fund is then used to provide pension and other benefits for the members when they fall due. The predominance of funded arrangements in the private sector stems from a condition of tax approval (see below) that arrangements should be set up under irrevocable trust, combined with the fact that setting assets aside in advance, separate from the assets of the employer, greatly enhances the security of members' rights.

Within the public sector, where the need to have a funded reserve is less, large schemes operate on an unfunded basis by which assets are not built up in advance of benefits coming into payment. These unfunded arrangements are established under statute. Although amendments are made from time to time under regulations, there is little if any scope for participating employers to tailor benefits to their own specification.

Final salary or money purchase

The basic concepts of final salary and money purchase schemes were outlined in Chapter 1. Fuller explanations are given below.

Final salary (defined benefit)

Under this benefit style, the member becomes entitled to a known pension benefit on retirement or leaving service. It is usual for the benefit to be based upon the member's salary at or approaching retirement date and his or her length of service within the scheme or with the employer. A wide range of definitions of salary may be used for this purpose, although the most common tends to be basic salary or total earnings in the year preceding retirement or averaged over a small number of years up to retirement.

A typical benefit structure would provide for a pension of 1/60 of final salary for each year of scheme membership, with part of the pension exchangeable ('commutable' in pensions terminology) for a tax-free lump sum. In the public sector, a pension of 1/80 *plus* a separate lump sum of 3/80 of final salary for each year of scheme membership has long been the norm.

Final salary arrangements give a degree of certainty of ultimate benefit to the member. Conversely, this also means that the employer bears the uncertainty of the ultimate cost of providing that benefit.

It is worth mentioning that besides the final salary scheme, there is a further design that falls within the defined benefit category. This is the average salary scheme, under which, as the name suggests, the benefit accrues as a percentage of average salary for the period of membership. Whilst currently very uncommon, there are occasional bouts of speculation that this design may gain in popularity.

Final salary has been the mainstream basis of UK pension provision and continues to be the preferred method of benefit delivery for many of the largest employers in the UK (though see Chapter 4).

Money purchase (defined contribution)

Under this system, all members have their own separately identifiable pension account within the scheme into which contributions from the member and the employer are paid. The account is invested to provide growth over the longer term; when the individual retires, the value of the account is used to provide pension and other benefits.

Clearly, the risk related to building up benefit rights in a money purchase scheme lies with the member. For the employer, costs are known and stable. Once a pension of a given amount is secured, the risk (of the member's longevity) transfers to the person paying the pension. Larger money purchase schemes may pay pensions directly themselves; most, however, will buy a pension policy (called an 'annuity') from an insurance company.

Occupational scheme or personal pension arrangement

A distinction needs to be drawn between occupational pension schemes directly organised and delivered by employers, and personal pension schemes where, although the employer may contribute, the contract is an individual one between the member and the provider, typically an insurance company or investment house.

In occupational schemes, there is frequent interaction between the trustees managing the scheme and the employer whose current and past employees are its members. An increasingly common arrangement is the group personal pension scheme, with terms agreed for the employees of a particular employer. Whilst it may be presented as a scheme in its own right, this is not strictly the case; it is merely a collecting arrangement for a series of individual contracts. The employer will have little involvement with the provider after inception of the arrangement. Technically, the employer's liability is restricted to deducting and paying across agreed employee and employer contributions within agreed timescales. However, it may invest heavily in communication, employer branding and employee awareness in order to give the feel of a distinctively separate employer-sponsored arrangement.

Tax-approved or unapproved

Pension schemes meeting detailed Inland Revenue requirements will qualify for a range of valuable tax reliefs in relation to contributions, investments and, to a lesser extent, benefits.

Tax-approved schemes

The vast majority of pension arrangements are set up on an 'approved' basis. This means that the scheme's rules and the way they are administered conform to the requirements of the Inland Revenue.

For occupational schemes, the requirements operate on the basis of defined limits on the emerging benefits payable by the scheme. These are mostly a function of remuneration in the years approaching retirement ('final remuneration') and length of service with the employer. A key point here is that schemes typically operate salary and, to a lesser extent, service definitions less generous than those allowed by the Inland Revenue. For instance, most schemes will not take full account of members' fluctuating earnings like bonuses, benefits in kind and allowances such as overtime. Similarly, schemes will usually only count years of service in the scheme towards the benefit formula, whilst the Inland Revenue will allow years of service with the employer to count. As the approval conditions have changed over time, a series of separate regimes have sprung up with different tax approval conditions applying to members according to the date they joined the scheme and the date the scheme was approved. This adds greatly to the complexity of administration.

For personal pension schemes, it is the contributions going in that are subject to limits. There are no monetary limits on the emerging benefits. Contributions up to £3,600 per annum (inclusive of basic rate tax relief) may be paid regardless of the member's earnings. Contributions above that level can be paid according to age- and earnings-related limits. These begin at 17.5 per cent of earnings for someone 35 or under at the beginning of the tax year and rise through a series of bands to 40 per cent of earnings for those aged 61 or over. To complicate matters further, money purchase occupational schemes that satisfy the prescribed criteria have been able from 6 April 2001 to seek approval on the personal pension basis (though instances of this happening are expected to be relatively rare).

Further consideration of the benefits that schemes can pay is given in Chapter 3.

The reason schemes bother to apply for Inland Revenue approval is to take advantage of the very valuable tax reliefs that it confers:

- Employee contributions are tax-deductible. On the occupational scheme basis, relief is given through the net pay arrangement (subject to a maximum employee contribution of 15 per cent of earnings). On the personal pension basis, employees' contributions are treated as paid net of basic rate tax; the provider automatically claims basic rate relief (which is added to the member's account), whilst it is for the member to reclaim any higher-rate relief through the end-of-year self-assessment tax return.

- The contributions paid by the employer are tax-deductible against corporation tax.
- Contributions paid by the employer in respect of an employee are not taxable on the employee as a benefit in kind.
- On death, lump sums under life cover arrangements can be paid to beneficiaries without incurring an inheritance tax liability.
- The assets in a scheme benefit from a tax-efficient environment. In particular, no income tax is payable on scheme investment income, and no capital gains tax is payable on gains arising from the disposal of investments.
- On retirement, part of the benefits may be paid as a tax-free cash sum.

Unapproved schemes

Mainstream benefit provision is by way of tax-approved arrangements. However, in some circumstances the employer may wish to provide a benefit that is greater than (or maybe different from) what is permissible within the tax-approved environment. In particular, employees who join an occupational scheme after 31 May 1989 have the remuneration counting for pension benefits limited to what is known as the earnings cap; similarly, the earnings of all members of personal pension schemes for contribution purposes are subject to the cap. In the 2001/02 tax year the earnings cap is £95,400. It is increased annually in line with retail price inflation (plus a small element of upward rounding); however, incomes historically have grown at a higher rate than prices, so the cap has an ever-increasing impact on approved benefits.

Individuals who are subject to the cap may have their earnings above the cap pensioned under an unapproved scheme. Most unapproved schemes are funded – giving rise to the acronym FURBS (funded unapproved retirement benefits schemes). Usually, FURBS operate on a money purchase basis, funded wholly by employer contributions. The member is taxed at his or her marginal rate of income tax on the value of employer contributions; National Insurance contributions are also payable on the contributions. The employer obtains corporation tax relief on contributions. Investment income is taxed at the lower and basic rates of income tax, whilst capital gains are taxed at 34 per cent. The benefit is paid as a tax-free lump sum on retirement. Although the tax burden on FURBS is greater than that on approved schemes, it is nonetheless likely to be lower than that on personally held investments.

Unfunded unapproved schemes are uncommon but are more suitable for replicating final salary promises. There are no contributions on which the member can be taxed, so it is the emerging benefit that is taxable. The growing benefit liability is reflected in the employer's accounts. Although efforts have been made to find ways to enhance members' security, unfunded arrangements have the particular drawback that the entitlement is dependent on the employer's still being in existence and able to pay the benefits at retirement.

Contracting out

Contracting out is an important and arguably unique feature of the UK's system of welfare.

The state earnings-related pension scheme (SERPS) was

introduced in 1978 and was designed to be a second-tier state-sponsored pension based upon the employee's career earnings history. It is operated on an unfunded basis and the costs are met from employer and employee National Insurance contributions.

In the absence of any other pension provision, membership of SERPS is compulsory. However, an employee may give up his or her right to SERPS and instead have a benefit in either an occupational or personal pension arrangement – this is called contracting out. SERPS is replaced from April 2002 by a new state second pension (S2P), providing more generous benefits for the lower paid. Contracting out will continue to operate in relation to S2P as it has done in relation to SERPS.

The incentive for giving up the SERPS/S2P entitlement is an effective reduction in the rate of National Insurance contributions payable by the employee and employer. The actual mechanism by which this reduction operates varies according to the type of scheme concerned.

As the state scheme benefit given up by contracting out is a state-sponsored arrangement with the associated guarantees of payment, stringent rules apply to give protection to the replacement contracted-out benefit. Contracting out can be achieved in one of three ways, depending on the structure chosen by the employer:

- by meeting a salary-related test under an occupational scheme
- by meeting a money purchase test under an occupational scheme
- by meeting a money purchase test under a personal pension scheme.

Contracted-out salary-related (COSR) schemes

Under a COSR scheme, the employee and employer pay a reduced rate of National Insurance contributions. In return, the scheme undertakes to provide a given level of benefit to replace the state scheme pension forgone. Unlike money purchase contracting out (see below), there is no direct link between the National Insurance reduction and the contributions paid into the scheme; as this is a defined benefit arrangement, the risk over time of the reduction not being sufficient to meet the cost of the benefits lies with the employer.

Until April 1997, a COSR scheme was obliged to offer a benefit entitlement called a guaranteed minimum pension (GMP). The GMP is calculated on a basis almost identical to the SERPS benefit given up. Since April 1997, no further GMP has built up (though existing GMP liabilities are still retained in the schemes in which they were built up). Instead, for a scheme to contract out on a COSR basis from April 1997 onwards, the scheme benefits are subject to an overall quality test, which operates by comparison against a hypothetical benchmark scheme – this is known as the reference scheme test.

Benefits must be broadly equivalent to or better than the reference scheme benefits if the scheme is to be able to contract out. Where a scheme has different categories of member, the test has to be applied to each category separately, with at least 90 per cent of members in each category able to pass the test.

The reference scheme test, although less specifically aligned to SERPS than the GMP, is nonetheless designed to ensure that the COSR scheme is, as a minimum, providing benefits broadly equivalent in value to the rights being given up.

Periodic tests must be made to ensure that the scheme continues to comply with the contracting-out requirements.

Contracted-out money purchase (COMP) schemes

Under a COMP scheme, the employer and employee pay a reduced rate of National Insurance contributions. A minimum level of contributions reflecting the reduction in National Insurance contributions is paid to the scheme by the employer to add to the member's separately identifiable pension account; this is further topped up after the end of each tax year by an additional age-related payment from the government. The money purchase rights that build up from these payments are called protected rights.

The member's protected rights fund must be used solely to buy a pension meeting particular conditions. These conditions vary slightly according to whether the rights were accrued before or after 6 April 1997. The key differences relate to the rate of pension increase payable and the fact that an unmarried member is no longer required to buy a spouse's pension. In all cases, the rate at which the fund is converted into pension cannot discriminate between men and women (ie unisex annuity rates must be used); also, the protected rights pension must come into payment between ages 60 and 75. As with a COSR scheme, there is ongoing supervision to ensure that the scheme continues to comply with the contracting-out requirements.

Because this is money-purchase-based contracting out, the member bears the risk of the COMP benefit falling short of what would have been payable under SERPS/S2P. Benefits arising from contributions over and above the minimum contracting-out payments are not subject to the strict protected rights criteria.

Contracted-out ('appropriate') personal pensions

Most personal pension contracts allow the member to choose to contract out. In this scenario, the employee and employer pay full-rate National Insurance contributions. The Inland Revenue then, after the end of the tax year, rebates part of the National Insurance contributions, together with an age-related top-up, to the member's personal pension plan. As with a COMP scheme, the protected rights fund derived from these payments must be used to buy a pension meeting prescribed conditions.

Scheme design issues

Whether or not to contract out and, if so, on what basis, is a key decision in pension planning. A central factor is that the contracting-out National Insurance rebate varies between COSR, COMP and appropriate personal pensions (APPs). For a start, the COSR rebate is flat-rate, whilst on both money purchase bases it is age-related. There are also differences between the COMP and APP rebates, with the APP rebates being higher to reflect factors such as the higher expenses payable under individual pension products.

It is also important to note that the contracting-out basis chosen need not be the same as the overall benefit structure of the occupational scheme. Thus a scheme that offers a final salary benefit may actually choose to contract out on a COMP basis; the protected rights benefit acts as an underpin, with the member being entitled to the final salary benefit or the protected rights pension, whichever is greater.

Schemes are able to contract out on both the COSR and COMP bases at the same time (if they are prepared to handle the administrative complexity). These are known as contracted-out mixed benefit (COMB) schemes. A member can only be contracted out under one arrangement at any one time, however.

With a COSR scheme, the member's employment is either contracted out or not: there is no element of individual choice. In a COMP scheme, being contracted out may be a condition of membership, although some schemes will allow members to make an individual choice as to whether they contract out. In an APP, the contracting out decision is entirely the member's. Clearly, where there is an element of personal choice, it is important that the member should take individual financial advice on the merits of contracting out. A member of an occupational scheme that is not contracted out is always able to contract out on his own initiative under a separate APP.

At the core of the contracting-out decision is the level of National Insurance rebate available. This is reviewed every five years, with the next change due from April 2002. On an individual level, the merits of contracting out tend to be highly age-sensitive. It is frequently possible to identify pivotal ages at which contracting out becomes, or ceases to be, a worthwhile proposition – though different analyses will always yield slightly different outcomes. For a COSR scheme, as a rule of thumb, contracting out is more worthwhile the younger the age profile of the overall membership. To prevent abuse of the system, legal measures have been introduced to discourage occupational schemes from switching the contracted-out status of their members at pivotal ages.

Stakeholder pensions

Anyone aware of developments on the UK pensions scene could be excused for wondering how they could have read so far without mention of this centrepiece of the Government's pensions reform programme.

Available to the public from 6 April 2001, stakeholder pensions represent an attempt to encourage those on middle incomes in particular to save more towards their own retirement. The intention was that stakeholder schemes should be characterised by simplicity, flexibility and value for money, although the extent to which these aims have been achieved is debatable.

A personal pension scheme or money purchase occupational scheme that meets stringent regulatory criteria is able to register as a stakeholder pension scheme. To this extent, a stakeholder scheme can be viewed merely as a personal or occupational pension scheme subject to an extra layer of regulation. The overwhelming majority of stakeholder schemes are established as personal pensions and references to personal pensions throughout this book can be taken to include stakeholder schemes. Occupational schemes seeking stakeholder status must be tax-approved under the personal pension tax regime discussed above.

The most important of the regulatory criteria are:

- a maximum annual charge of 1 per cent of the member's fund
- minimum contributions, whether one-off or regular, to be set no higher than £20
- detailed annual statements about the member's own pension account and about the way the scheme has been administered

- members to be offered a default investment choice (ie they cannot be forced to make a decision about investments).

It is worth noting that the equation of stakeholder schemes with personal pensions does not hold good in the following areas:

- contracting-out rebates – the government has the power to set separate rebates for stakeholder schemes; however, for the time being, it has chosen not to do so; a stakeholder scheme set up as a personal pension will receive personal pension rebates; a stakeholder scheme set up as an occupational scheme will receive the COMP rebate
- employer access – employers must offer their employees access to a stakeholder scheme unless specified alternative provision is in place; this is discussed in more detail in Chapter 7
- financial services regulation – the rules governing the sale and marketing of schemes registered as stakeholder are less strict than those governing personal pension schemes without stakeholder accreditation.

What benefits can an occupational scheme provide?

> ☑ Member's pension
> ☑ Tax-free lump sum
> ☑ Spouse's and dependants' pensions
> ☑ Lump sums on death
>   Death before retirement
>   Death after retirement
> ☑ Incapacity

The types of benefit that a tax-approved occupational pension scheme can provide, and their amount, are limited by the requirements of the Inland Revenue. This chapter provides an overview of the restrictions.

Member's pension

The pension payable to the member at the scheme's normal retirement age is clearly at the heart of the benefit entitlement. A career maximum pension of ⅔ of final remuneration is the overall Inland Revenue limit. However, apart from executives who are able to secure a high level of employer funding, few members will achieve this level. Sometimes it is necessary to restrict members' pensions to take account of benefits built up in previous employments or periods of self-employment.

Scheme rules can allow an early retirement pension to be paid from age 50 onwards. Usually this will be reduced to reflect the fact that it is coming into payment early. Conversely, a member may be able to defer payment of the pension until after normal retirement age, in which case it will usually be enhanced for late payment.

A member leaving service before normal retirement age who has completed at least two years' service in the scheme is entitled to have his or her benefit preserved until retirement age. (Scheme rules may, but do not have to, grant leavers with less than two years' service a refund of their own contributions. Equally, they may offer to preserve the benefit, though this is rare.) Final salary scheme leavers must also have their preserved pension increased by the lesser of 5 per cent per annum compound and the increase in retail prices over the period to normal retirement age. (Money purchase members just benefit from fund growth.) As this protection has been repeatedly strengthened since its introduction in 1975, many schemes will still have deferred members to whom lesser levels of protection apply.

Once a pension is in payment, it must continue for life. (An exception to this is where a member retires before state pension age and the scheme is designed to pay a temporary 'bridging' pension to help him or her until the state pension comes into payment.) Payments on pension rights built up since 6 April 1997 must, as a *minimum*, increase each year by the lesser of 5 per cent and the increase in retail prices. This basis is known as 'limited price indexation' (LPI). The *maximum* increase allowed by the Inland Revenue, on the other hand, is the greater of 3 per cent per annum compound and the increase in the retail prices index.

Further conditions apply to contracted-out pensions.

Tax-free lump sum

It is standard for schemes to allow members to take a tax-free lump sum on retirement, either by commuting part of the pension or as a separate entitlement. The maximum is 1½ times final remuneration. For members joining a scheme after 16 March 1987, the maximum lump sum entitlement is tied directly to the amount of pension actually payable to the member. Of course, scheme rules may not always allow members to take the maximum lump sum allowed by the Inland Revenue.

Spouse's and dependants' pensions

Whether the member dies before or after retirement, a pension can be paid to his or her legal spouse and anyone who was financially dependent on the member at the date of death. Scheme rules may define the class of beneficiary more narrowly than the Inland Revenue allows, so this always needs to be checked.

The benefit itself will usually be expressed as either a percentage of the member's pension at the date of death, a percentage of the maximum pension that could have been payable to the member at the normal retirement date, or a fraction (eg $\frac{1}{20}$) of the member's salary at the date of death for each year of pensionable service.

The Inland Revenue maximum for a spouse's or dependant's pension is ⅔ of the maximum potential pension that could have been paid to the member at normal retirement age. If more than one such pension is payable, the total must not exceed the member's maximum potential pension. On death after retirement, the maximum potential pension can be increased in line with the retail prices index for the period after normal retirement age.

Spouses' and dependants' pensions are subject to LPI (limited price indexation) increases in payment, to the extent that they relate to the member's service after 5 April 1997. This may not be easy to work out under some benefit structures. The maximum increases are as for the member's own pension (see above).

When a member retires, his or her pension may be guaranteed for up to 10 years. Where this is the case and the member dies within the guarantee period, the pension continues in payment to the spouse or dependants. If the guarantee was for no more than five years, the remaining instalments can be paid as a lump sum free of inheritance tax. The recipient may be decided at the trustees' discretion and is not limited to the spouse and financial dependants. Again, however, the scheme rules may apply a more restrictive class of beneficiary than the Inland Revenue permits.

Lump sums on death

Death before retirement

If a member dies before retirement, the scheme can pay a lump sum of up to four times final remuneration to one or more beneficiaries chosen at the trustees' discretion. Usually a member will be asked to complete an 'expression of wish', stating to whom he or she would like the benefit to be paid. However, in order to avoid inheritance tax on the payments, it is important that the trustees are not bound by this. (Usually, they will closely follow the member's wishes, but they must have discretion.) The Inland Revenue places no restriction on the class of beneficiaries for these payments, though the scheme rules may well do so. Trustees should be prepared to undertake investigations into the personal circumstances of deceased members in order to identify appropriate beneficiaries, not just rely on the expression of wish alone.

This kind of life cover is common for scheme members who are still in service with the employer. For those who have left but have a deferred pension in the scheme, life cover is more of a rarity.

Death after retirement

The rules governing schemes' ability to offer life cover after a member has retired are quite complex. There is nothing to stop a scheme offering a nominal lump sum on death of up to £2,500 (often referred to as a funeral grant) in respect of any retired member, distributed at the trustees' discretion. However, payments over and above that level are largely prohibited for members who joined the scheme after 30 September 1991. Where payment is allowed, it can only be paid to the member's spouse or estate and is within the scope of inheritance tax.

Incapacity

Schemes can allow a member to retire at any age on grounds of incapacity. The scheme's definition of incapacity must be within the terms set by the Inland Revenue – ie physical or mental deterioration that is sufficiently serious to prevent the individual from following his or her normal employment, or which seriously impairs his or her earning ability.

For incapacity, a more generous benefit may be granted than for other forms of early retirement. The Inland Revenue will allow a pension and tax-free lump sum to be paid as if the member had stayed in service until normal retirement age (ie taking account of prospective future service).

Rejected claims for incapacity pensions are a frequent cause of complaint by members. It is particularly important for trustees to familiarise themselves with the provisions of their own scheme rules and to follow the procedures (eg on taking medical advice) carefully, documenting how they have reached the decision to pay or not to pay incapacity benefits.

As an alternative to offering enhanced early retirement benefits from a pension scheme, many employers offer permanent health insurance (PHI). This is an insurance policy that pays an income to someone who has been taken ill with a long-term illness or disability. PHI policies cannot be held within approved occupational pension schemes.

What are the current trends and influences on pension provision?

- ✔ Europe
- ✔ The squeeze on final salary schemes
  - Demographics
  - The minimum funding requirement
  - Regulation
  - Accounting standard FRS17

Europe

A key element in recent years has been European Union legislation. This has been felt most keenly in the sphere of sex equality. A succession of test cases at the European Court of Justice has swept away the long-standing norm of different retirement ages for men and women and made it clear that both access to pension schemes and the benefits they provide must be offered on the same basis to men and women.

The issue of equal access has been highlighted most prominently in the case of part-time workers. Until the early 1990s, it had been the common practice of many employers to exclude part-timers from pension scheme membership; because in most cases the proportion of women in the part-time workforce is greater than that in the full-time workforce, excluding part-timers in this way discriminates indirectly against women. Unless an employer can demonstrate objective justification for the exclusion, such discrimination is unlawful. The most recent cases addressing this issue have established that part-timers may be able to claim retrospective membership of their employer's scheme as far back as April 1976 (the date of an earlier test case). Other excluded groups, such as fixed-term contract workers, may be able to establish claims along similar lines.

A few lawful exceptions to the equal treatment principle have been established. These relate primarily to the mortality assumptions underpinning certain calculations in final salary schemes. As far as money purchase schemes are concerned, it remains an untested though vitally important assumption that provided contributions to the scheme are equal for men and women, it is okay at retirement to convert the members' funds to pension at different rates for men and women.

There are continuing doubts as to whether contracted-out rights in the form of guaranteed minimum pensions are lawful in terms of sex equality (since the scheme's terms are obliged to reflect unequal state pension ages). Whilst the likelihood is that they are not, case law has so far failed to clarify this adequately. The problem for employers with all sex discrimination findings is that they require equalisation at the higher male or female level, with major resultant cost implications.

UK regulations that came into force on 1 July 2000 (to

satisfy the European Union Part-Time Workers Directive) tie up most of the loose ends of the part-timers issue by making it unlawful to treat part-timers less favourably than comparable full-timers as regards their terms and conditions of employment (unless this can be justified objectively). This is tested on a pro rata basis, according to hours worked. This removes the need for an employee to demonstrate indirect sex discrimination. However, the pro rata stipulation makes it almost impossible to justify the hitherto common practice of making a flat-rate deduction from members' pensions to reflect the fact that they are assumed to be receiving the basic state pension. Most schemes are now either withdrawing this practice (known as 'integration', or 'clawback' to the trade unions that have long campaigned against it) or adjusting it so that a pro-rata deduction is made for part-timers.

New European legislation is being introduced to improve the rights of workers on fixed-term contracts. Whilst this will not oblige the UK government to give contract workers equal pension rights to permanent workers, the government has consulted on the possibility of doing so unilaterally.

The squeeze on final salary schemes

Over the past decade, it has been possible to identify an accelerating trend away from final salary schemes towards money purchase arrangements, whether occupational or personal pensions. The reasons for this are varied; many affect all types of provision.

Demographics

People are living longer. This means that pensions have to be paid over an increasingly long period, making them ever more expensive. A final salary scheme could take account of this for future service by raising its retirement age, worsening future benefits or increasing employee contributions. For past service benefits, however, this extra cost is borne by the employer. In a money purchase scheme, as we have seen, such risks are borne by the members. Finance directors keen to control costs are not oblivious to this fact.

Further, a trend towards greater job mobility is also argued to favour money purchase provision.

The minimum funding requirement

Approved final salary schemes must meet a statutory funding standard known as the minimum funding requirement (MFR). This is intended to ensure that if a scheme discontinues, it will be able to secure benefits on a prescribed basis. Unfortunately, the MFR supposes a certain level of return on investments that has not been met in practice (through no fault of the schemes – largely a result of the falling level of dividends). The time limits for restoring funding to the statutory level are very tight. Again, the result is increased cost for the sponsoring employer.

For all this, the MFR has provided little reassurance to members or trustees. It is too complicated and its very name is misleading. Given its shortcomings, the government has announced its intended abolition but due to the need to find parliamentary time to put in place a replacement (intended to be more closely geared to the circumstances of each individual scheme) it is likely to continue in force until at least 2003.

Regulation

The Pensions Act 1995 introduced a range of measures to protect the security of occupational scheme members' benefit rights. The majority of these requirements affect final salary schemes disproportionately; money purchase occupational schemes gain many exemptions (whilst personal pensions are scarcely touched by the Act). Compliance with the Act has greatly increased scheme administration and the need for scheme trustees and employers to take professional advice – and hence has increased cost.

Accounting standard FRS17

FRS17 is the new accounting standard for pension costs. When fully implemented in 2003, occupational scheme assets and liabilities will have to be measured at market value and the resulting surplus or deficit recognised immediately on the company balance sheet. With final salary schemes, this will cause the balance sheet figures to fluctuate greatly from year to year. This may cause all kinds of problems for companies. At the extreme, dividends could be hit due to there being insufficient reserves to pay them. Where a business's main competitor has a money purchase scheme, the competitor's balance sheet will remain stable; this may create an unfavourable comparison with the company running a final salary scheme.

These factors are combining to encourage many sponsors of final salary schemes either to close those schemes to new entrants or to wind them up altogether. They are typically being replaced by money purchase arrangements, whether occupational schemes or, for minimal employer involvement, group personal pensions.

How do we deliver and administer schemes?

- ✔ Insured package
- ✔ Self-administered by a third party
- ✔ Self-administered in-house
- ✔ So what to choose? – Is it a matter of size?

As we have seen earlier in this guide, occupational schemes are generally established under trust; this is a legal structure that gives members rights to certain benefits and gives trustees – who look after the pension scheme – certain responsibilities. These responsibilities include ensuring that funds are invested properly and that benefits paid to members are paid on time, correctly and to the right individuals – the cornerstone of good administration.

The trust deed (setting out administrative provisions) and rules (setting out membership, contribution and benefit provisions) are the legal wrapper from which pensions are delivered. To deliver schemes, certain fundamentals of investment of the scheme contributions and assets are needed, together with basic record-keeping and the payment of benefits. There is also a need for appropriate advice to ensure the operation of the scheme keeps up to date with trends in pensions and changes in legislation. With these factors in mind, employers can choose various ways to operate their scheme. These can be summarised as:

- insured package
- self-administered by a third party
- self-administered in-house.

It is important to be clear here that we are talking about the means of day-to-day administration. In all cases, trustees will be sitting over and above the administrative structure, with ultimate responsibility for the scheme's operation.

Insured package

A packaged insured scheme is one in which, at the risk of tautology, all services are provided by an insurance company in one overall package. This means that the insurance company provides the record-keeping and administration services, including the settling of benefits. Other services within the package include the collection of contributions and investment of the scheme assets by the insurer's investment management arm. The scheme invests solely in insurance policies.

The insurer also provides documentation to enable the scheme to be set up, and liaises with the Inland Revenue to obtain and maintain the tax-approved status of the scheme.

Self-administered by a third party

Schemes operating on this basis have split out the various component parts of scheme operation in such a way that the scheme is not operated on a packaged approach and services are typically not provided by an insurer. Investments will normally include assets other than insurance policies.

Record-keeping and administration is typically undertaken by a specialist firm. This may or may not be the same firm that provides actuarial and benefit consultancy services, and that will also assist the trustees in selecting an investment manager to invest and manage the scheme's assets. The investment manager may possibly be the investment management arm of an insurance company but is equally likely to be a specialist investment house.

The trust deed and rules and associated documentation are provided by a specialist pensions lawyer. The obtaining of tax approval with the Inland Revenue would be undertaken by the benefit consultancy.

Self-administered in-house

This type of management can take on various forms.

By in-house we mean the employing company providing directly the functions of pension scheme operation, in the same way as it has a specialist HR department, finance department, marketing department and so on. There are various degrees by which this can be done.

In its simplest format, in-house administration means an employer taking on only the member record-keeping and benefit administration, with all other services being provided externally through specialists as described in the self-administered basis above. Quite often the establishment of an administration team in-house is accompanied by the appointment of a pensions manager who will have similar skills to a consultant in a benefits consultancy and who is able to advise the company and trustees on trends, legislative developments and other pensions issues.

A handful of the very largest schemes have their own specialist team dealing with the investment management of the scheme assets.

So what to choose? – Is it a matter of size?

Typically, smaller schemes will find the insured package approach suitable for them. The insurance company provides economies of scale in terms of all the fundamental work that goes into the establishment and operation of systems. Typically, a scheme of fewer than 100 members would be administered in this manner.

Above perhaps 200 members, the self-administered basis becomes clearly more appropriate. This is on the grounds of cost saving and the fact that as a scheme becomes bigger (reflecting the size of the sponsoring company), the needs of the scheme will tend to diverge from the average and will begin to generate a need for certain features to be tailored to its own particular circumstances. This is something that a self-administered basis can provide but an insured package has limited scope to do. Membership size is not the be-all and end-all, because a scheme with a relatively small number of members may have considerable assets. For example, a £10,000,000 fund might, on an insured package basis, have annual charges of perhaps £100,000 to £150,000 per annum (ie 1–1½ per cent of the assets). A scheme of this fund size could plausibly have as few as 150 to 200 members and, on a self-administered basis, is likely to cost much less than £100,000 per annum to administer.

Due to factors such as the fixed costs of buying in specialist software packages, taking administration in-house becomes financially viable only as the scheme membership heads towards 10,000. Cost is not, of course, the only issue in taking administration in-house and the additional risk aspect must be taken into account. These risks include the recruitment and retention of specialist staff combined with the fact that any errors in the calculation of benefits would fall upon the employer as opposed to the benefits consultancy providing those services.

What are the duties and responsibilities of trustees?

- ✔ The trustee body
- ✔ Regulatory bodies
    - The Occupational Pensions Regulatory Authority (Opra)
    - Inland Revenue
    - Pension Schemes Registry
    - Information Commissioner
    - Pensions Ombudsman
- ✔ Advisers
    - Scheme actuary
    - Accountant
    - Scheme auditor
    - Investment manager
    - Custodians
    - Pensions consultants
    - Lawyers
- ✔ Administering the trust
    - Decision-making
    - Books and records
    - Bank account
- ✔ Dispute resolution
- ✔ Disclosure of information

Generic information

Individual information

☑ Transfer values

☑ Divorce

Earmarking

Sharing

☑ Sex equality

☑ Contributions and funding issues

☑ Statement of investment principles

☑ Self-investment

☑ Discontinuance

The basic role of pension scheme trustees is to administer the scheme according to its trust deed and rules, and within the law, in the best interests of its beneficiaries. Beneficiaries will include active, deferred and pensioner members of the scheme, together with spouses and dependants of deceased members; the sponsoring employer may, in some circumstances, be considered a beneficiary also.

The law governing trustees is a mixture of trust law that has developed over a period of centuries and, increasingly, statutory law (Acts of Parliament backed up by highly detailed sets of regulations) aimed at codifying particular requirements for pension schemes. The most significant element of statute is the Pensions Act 1995. This sets out many of the requirements described below and aims to enforce the principle that every breach of a requirement should carry a penalty; these mostly civil penalties are not spelled out below but they are there, lurking in the background.

There are many exemptions from the detailed measures described in this chapter. Considerations of space prevent any detailed exposition of these but they frequently cover unapproved schemes, schemes providing benefits only on death, and schemes for senior executives who will be able to exert significant control or influence over their pension arrangements.

The trustee body

The trustee body can be either a board composed of individual trustees, a single corporate trustee in which individuals serve as directors, or a trust corporation providing trustee services on a commercial basis. (Sometimes a combination of these may be employed.) Whichever constitution is chosen, the trustees' duties and the way they work are essentially the same. References to 'trustees' throughout this guide should be taken to include directors of corporate trustees.

Legislation gives scheme members the right to select one-third of the trustee body ('member-nominated trustees'). However, the employer is able to opt out of this provision by submitting alternative arrangements for members' approval (under prescribed consultation arrangements).

The trust documents will normally specify the terms of office of trustees and conditions for their appointment and removal.

An independent trustee must be appointed to a final salary scheme if the employer becomes insolvent. The appointment is the responsibility of the insolvency practitioner. Certain scheme powers are reserved to this independent trustee.

Whilst in general anyone can become a trustee, certain persons are disqualified. These include:

- anyone disqualified or suspended by Opra, the pensions regulator (see below)
- the scheme auditor and actuary (see below)
- those with unspent convictions involving dishonesty or deception
- undischarged bankrupts
- those disqualified from acting as a company director.

Regulatory bodies

In the course of their duties, trustees can expect to have to report to or liaise with a variety of regulatory bodies. The main ones are described below.

The Occupational Pensions Regulatory Authority (Opra)

Opra was set up under the Pensions Act 1995 to help ensure that pension schemes are secure and well run. It has a wide range of powers and sanctions, including: prohibiting and disqualifying trustees; imposing fines; appointing new trustees to schemes in difficulty.

There are no routine reports that trustees have to make to Opra – it is a reactive regulator. However, there are situations, notably failure to pay due contributions, where trustees have a legal obligation to report to Opra. They also have the right to report to Opra, as does any other person involved in the scheme administration, if they believe that other trustees, employers or professional advisers are not meeting the legal requirements on the way the scheme is run.

Opra publishes many guides that are invaluable to trustees in discharging their duties.

Inland Revenue

The Inland Revenue Savings, Pensions, Share Schemes division deals with applications for tax approval. It also monitors ongoing compliance with benefit limits and other tax approval requirements (many of which are applied under discretionary powers). Regular periodic reports by trustees include an annual return showing chargeable events under the scheme and reviews of funding, varying according to the nature of the scheme (eg for self-administered schemes, normally an actuarial valuation at least once in every 3½ years).

Applications to contract out and ongoing monitoring of compliance of contracted-out schemes are dealt with by the National Insurance Contributions Office of the Inland Revenue (see Chapter 2).

Self-administered schemes are required to submit an annual self-assessment tax return.

Pension Schemes Registry

This body is run by Opra. Trustees must register their scheme, providing specified pieces of information. These include: names and addresses of the trustees; employers (past and present); the number of members; the benefit basis. Annual updates are required.

The Registry also collects two annual levies: a general levy to cover the cost of Opra, and a compensation levy to fund a compensation scheme covering certain losses to occupational schemes caused by unlawful removal of assets from the schemes of insolvent employers. The size of the general levy increases according to the number of scheme members; the compensation levy is flat-rate but has not actually been levied in recent years (because the compensation scheme has very rarely been called upon to pay out).

Information Commissioner

The Information Commissioner (formerly the Data Protection Commissioner) is the supervisory authority for information-handling by those who process personal data concerning identifiable, living individuals. Since pension scheme trustees fall into this class of data controller they must register with ('notify') the Commissioner and abide by complex legislation governing the use of personal data. There is no ongoing compliance monitoring but the notification does have to be renewed annually.

Pensions Ombudsman

The Ombudsman's role is to investigate and decide upon complaints alleging injustice through maladministration, and also disputes of fact or law. In practice, most cases are brought by members against the trustees or employer. However, the Ombudsman's jurisdiction does extend to cases brought between trustees and employers. There is no systematic interaction between trustees and the Ombudsman; it occurs as and when cases arise.

Advisers

Trustees have a duty to take advice on technical and other matters that they do not fully understand.

The scheme trust deed should contain provisions for appointing advisers and usually also detail how they are to be remunerated, eg with the trustees paying the fees and then being reimbursed by the employer.

Under the Pensions Act 1995 certain advisers have to be appointed and specific letters of appointment have to be exchanged. These letters and agreements must include what happens in the event of conflicts of interest. There are specific provisions on the removal and resignation of professional advisers under these statutory provisions.

There are also times when there is a failure in the scheme, and professional advisers must by law report such occurrences to the regulatory authorities. This 'whistleblowing' requirement is designed to make advisers raise concerns on the financial or operational strength of the scheme independently of the trustees and employer (who might have motives for concealing deficiencies).

Detailed below are the main advisers trustees either have to appoint by law or can appoint to assist in the operation of the pension scheme.

Scheme actuary

A scheme actuary is required to be appointed for a final salary scheme. The scheme has to be valued under the minimum funding requirement provisions (see Chapter 4) at least once every three years. The basic valuation process looks at the ability of the scheme to provide the accrued benefit entitlements, and calculates required contribution rates.

(The employer will also require actuarial input to comply with accounting standards for pension costs.)

Accountant

Good financial records of a scheme are essential, as they form the basis on which the accounts for audit are prepared. The accounts include not only the day-to-day movements of contribution and benefit payments but also the movements in assets of the scheme from sales, purchases and investment income.

Scheme auditor

An appointed scheme auditor is a statutory requirement. Obviously the main duty is to audit the scheme accounts, which the trustees must have done within seven months of the scheme year-end.

Investment manager

Trustees of self-administered schemes must appoint investment managers for the day-to-day management of the scheme's investments.

An investment consultant may also be appointed to advise on the wider strategy for scheme investment and to help select and monitor the investment managers.

Custodians

When individual investments are held, custodians are appointed for safe-keeping of the scheme assets. Their duties also include proper settlement of purchases and sales, and claiming dividends and tax credits due to the scheme.

Pensions consultants

The legislation surrounding pension schemes is ever changing, as are other influences on scheme design and practice. Trustees have to be certain that they are aware of these developments and implement any changes required correctly and on time. A pension consultant will advise the trustees on such developments and may co-ordinate the services of the trustees' other advisers.

Lawyers

Appointment of a lawyer is not mandatory, but is required when trustees seek legal advice, for instance on complex issues of interpretation, particularly where disputes have arisen.

Administering the trust

There are very few hard-and-fast rules as to how the trustees go about their day-to-day scheme business. Three important requirements are considered below.

Decision-making

Legislation provides that trustees' decisions can be taken by majority vote, unless the scheme rules say otherwise. Where decisions are taken by majority, the trustees can agree a quorum (again, unless the rules say otherwise). Unless there is particular urgency, at least 10 business days' notice must be given of any meeting at which majority decisions may be taken.

Books and records

Trustees must keep proper books and records. Legislation requires that these include:

- records of meetings, including:
  - date, time and place
  - trustees invited and trustees attending
  - other attendees
  - decisions made
  - any other occasions since the previous meeting when trustees have taken a decision

- records of transactions, including:
  - contributions received
  - dates of members' joining
  - payments of benefits
  - payments or transfers of assets to any other person (eg professional advisers)
  - transfer values into and out of the scheme
  - payments to the employer.

These books and records must be kept for at least six years (though frequently it will be prudent to keep them much longer).

Bank account

Trustees must keep any money received by them in a bank account separate from the employer.

Dispute resolution

Trustees must operate a two-stage internal dispute resolution procedure to resolve disputes raised by members. Regulations prescribe key features that the procedure must follow at each stage.

Disclosure of information

Trustees must provide prescribed information to members (and sometimes other beneficiaries, prospective members and recognised trade unions) in specified circumstances. Sometimes this is only on request but in some cases it is automatic; in all cases there are set time limits for providing information. The information can be broken down into broad generic and member-specific categories.

Generic information

The main items are:

- scheme documents (eg the trust deed)
- basic scheme information and changes thereto (eg an outline of membership, contribution and benefit conditions)
- a scheme annual report and other periodically produced documents (eg actuarial valuation)
- information about certain key events (eg scheme discontinuance and failures to pay correct/timely contributions).

Individual information

The time limits for many of these statements are triggered by events of which the trustees may be unaware unless notified by the employer. Systems must be in place to make sure that exchange of information is triggered automatically when relevant events occur (eg death of a member). Key mediums of information include:

- annual benefit statements
- benefit statements when benefits become payable
- statement of beneficiaries' rights and options on the member's death
- statement of rights and options of members leaving service
- statements relating to transfer values.

Transfer values

Members whose benefits have not come into payment generally have a right to transfer the value of their benefits to another occupational or personal pension scheme. Legislation sets out a minimum 'cash equivalent' basis for calculating transfer values. There are strict time limits for payment. The regulatory details vary considerably for final salary and money purchase schemes.

Divorce

Divorce courts are obliged to take into account the value of the parties' pension rights. They can do this in one of three ways:

- offsetting the pension rights against other marital assets
- applying an earmarking order
- applying a sharing order.

All three require the trustees to provide a valuation of pension rights (on a cash equivalent basis). The last two require a greater level of involvement from the trustees, both in the provision of information and administration.

Earmarking

An earmarking order requires the trustees to pay part or all of the member's pension, retirement lump sum or death-in-service lump sum directly to the member's former spouse. The pension is still strictly the member's legal entitlement and is taxed according to his or her tax code. The drawback is that earmarking does not provide a 'clean break', largely in that the pension continues until the member dies.

Sharing

A pension sharing order requires the trustees to take away part of the member's pension rights and establish pension rights of equivalent value for the former spouse. They can do this within their own scheme or by transferring the former spouse's new rights to another pension arrangement. Pension sharing does offer a clean break but is complicated when it comes down to detail.

Trustees will see both earmarking and sharing orders in draft form but will only have a very limited time to comment. Orders should be checked carefully to make sure that they can actually be implemented by the scheme; experience has shown that many are badly worded.

Sex equality

Some of the key sex equality issues stemming from the European Union were discussed in Chapter 4. The implications of successive European test cases were codified in UK pensions legislation, under the Pensions Act 1995. This requires trustees to operate their scheme as if it contained an 'equal treatment rule' requiring access and benefit terms to be equal for men and women. Exercise of trustees' discretion must also conform to this principle.

Contributions and funding issues

Trustees must maintain a schedule showing the rates and due dates of contributions due. In final salary schemes, this is known as a 'schedule of contributions'; in money purchase schemes it is a 'payments schedule'.

Members have a right to pay additional voluntary contributions to the scheme to buy benefits over and above their normal scheme entitlement. These do not have to be included on either form of schedule.

Failure by the employer to pay in accordance with the schedule must (with prescribed exceptions for minor breaches) be reported by the trustees to Opra. Trustees should therefore establish clear procedures for payment in co-operation with the employer.

In final salary schemes, the amounts set out in the schedule are designed to ensure that the scheme meets the minimum funding requirement referred to in Chapter 4. The amounts on the schedule must be certified by the scheme actuary as being adequate for this purpose.

The flip side to the minimum funding requirement is the range of measures imposed by the Inland Revenue to ensure that the money paid into the scheme is not excessive in relation to the benefits promised. The detailed tests are set out in a combination of legislation and published discretionary practice.

Statement of investment principles

Trustees of most schemes must maintain a written statement of investment principles, explaining how they invest the scheme's assets. The statement must cover prescribed issues, including the kind of investments the scheme holds, the trustees' attitude to risk and the expected return on investments.

Self-investment

Trustees may not invest more than 5 per cent of the scheme's assets in investments relating to the sponsoring employer or its associates. These include: shares; land used by or leased to the employer; property connected with the employer's business. Loans to the employer and its associates are entirely prohibited (including debentures).

Discontinuance

The power to discontinue a scheme will normally lie with the employer, though the precise mechanism by which this is brought about will be spelled out in the rules. Whilst it is sometimes desirable to keep the scheme going without any further contributions or benefits accruing (running a 'closed scheme'), it is more often the case that the trustees will be required to wind it up completely by liquidating the assets and using them to secure members' benefits elsewhere.

Where a scheme winds up, the rules will specify a priority order, setting out which classes of benefit must be secured first (eg pensions in payment, contracted-out rights and so on). This is less of an issue in money purchase schemes and is of limited importance in final salary schemes that have enough assets to meet all their liabilities in full. It is, however, crucial where the assets fall short of being able to buy full benefits for all members. In final salary schemes that started winding up after 5 April 1997, the scheme's own priority order is overridden by a statutory priority order.

In final salary schemes, a winding up shortfall between the scheme's assets and liabilities calculated on the minimum funding requirement basis becomes a debt due from the employer to the trustees.

Conversely, if there are surplus assets left after the trustees have secured scheme benefits in full, it may be possible to make a payment to the employer. However, there are onerous regulatory hurdles to overcome before this can be done.

Winding up is a particularly difficult area, giving rise to a need for much specialist advice.

What are an employer's responsibilities in respect of pensions?

- ✔ Taking on a new employee
- ✔ Stakeholder pensions
- ✔ Scheme rules: the balance of powers
- ✔ Disclosing information
- ✔ Paying contributions
- ✔ Paying benefits
- ✔ Employee trustees

There is no codified set of rules for employers where pension schemes are concerned. The following paragraphs pick out some of the main areas to look out for.

Taking on a new employee

Legislation requires that there is a reference to pensions in an employee's written statement of terms of employment, even if it is a negative statement.

Once the scheme trustees are aware of a new member or

potential new member, it is legally their responsibility to furnish further information about the scheme.

Personnel practitioners would be well advised to think very carefully before making any one-off benefit promises to new recruits (or to amend the entitlement of existing employees) without checking that the pension scheme rules will allow it and that the scheme administrators will be able to administer it.

Stakeholder pensions

There has hitherto been no requirement for employers to become involved in pension provision. This changes from 8 October 2001, with the coming into force of a stakeholder pensions access requirement.

This requires all employers with more than four employees to provide access to a stakeholder pension scheme for all their employees who cannot join an occupational pension scheme or a qualifying group personal pension scheme. (Broadly, to satisfy the personal pension exemption criteria, the employer must be contributing at least 3 per cent of basic pay, the scheme must levy no charges on members who leave or transfer their funds elsewhere, and it must be available to employees on these terms as of right.) Those within three months of starting employment and those whose earnings have not risen above the National Insurance lower earnings limit for any week in the previous three months do not have to be given access.

Providing access requires consulting the employees who will be able to join the stakeholder pension scheme about the choice of scheme, providing them with contact details, and paying over their contributions by payroll deduction.

The employer itself does not have to contribute and, to limit administration, can place certain restrictions on the frequency with which employees change the amounts of their contributions. Failure to abide by the access requirements can result in fines of up to £50,000.

Scheme rules: the balance of powers

The trust deed and rules of most schemes will contain powers to agree certain courses of action. These are likely to include the power to amend the scheme, to increase ('augment') benefits, to agree incapacity and other early retirement pensions, and to wind up the scheme. The way these powers are shared between the trustees and employer is referred to as the balance of powers and varies from scheme to scheme. Employers need to know which powers are theirs to exercise and must bear in mind that some powers may be fiduciary powers – they must be exercised in good faith towards the members, with the employer acting in a trustee-like way.

The employer normally has power to stop contributing to the scheme, usually prompting its discontinuance.

Legislation may override scheme rules to take away powers. For instance, an employer cannot exercise a power to refund scheme surplus monies to itself; to do so is a civil offence. Similarly, scheme rules cannot validly require employer consent to any scheme investment decisions.

Disclosing information

An employer must disclose to the trustees on request any information they or their advisers reasonably need to perform their duties. Also, without being asked, the employer must tell the trustees within one month of any event relating to the employer that might be of material significance to them in performing their duties.

Paying contributions

Where an employer is deducting employees' pension contributions from payroll and paying them to a pension scheme of any kind, they must be received by the scheme no later than the nineteenth day of the month following that in which they were deducted from pay. Fraudulent failure to pay in a timely fashion is a criminal offence; lesser failures are a civil offence. (An apparently slight but, in practice, important variation on this is that an employer paying National Insurance rebates to a COMP scheme must do so within 14 days of the end of the *tax* month to which they relate – ie also by the nineteenth day but crucially different where payroll is run in the first five days of the month.)

As mentioned in Chapter 6, occupational scheme trustees must maintain a schedule showing the rates and due dates of employee and employer contributions. It is the employer's responsibility to pay in line with the schedule. For money purchase pension schemes, it is a civil offence not to pay contributions by the legal due dates set out in the schedule. For salary-related pension schemes, the rules are more complex but overdue contributions become a formal debt due from the employer to the trustees.

Unlike occupational schemes, with a personal pension (including stakeholder) scheme, it is the employer's responsibility to maintain a schedule showing the rates and due dates of contributions and to pay in line with that schedule.

The scheme provider must have an up-to-date version at all times and is required to report to Opra any slip-up, however slight.

Paying benefits

In some cases, the employer may be responsible for paying over benefits from the scheme to the members. Where this is the case, any monies not paid over within two business days of receipt by the employer must be put into a separate bank account until they are paid.

Employee trustees

Scheme trustees who are employees must be allowed reasonable time off work – paid – to carry out trustee duties and to undergo training for those duties. Also, the employer cannot subject an employee to any detriment on the grounds of the employee's trustee activities.

An employee who is a trustee or who is involved in pension scheme administration cannot be sued by the employer for breach of confidence if he or she makes a report to Opra regarding some breach of duty concerning the scheme.

How do we communicate pension arrangements to our employees?

- ☑ Why does it matter?
- ☑ Where do we start?
- ☑ Brochures and booklets
- ☑ Presentations
- ☑ Surgeries
- ☑ Pensions helpline
- ☑ Benefit statements
- ☑ Local pensions officers (LPOs)
- ☑ Intranet
- ☑ Have we succeeded?

Why does it matter?

Employers spend large sums on providing occupational pension schemes. Costs often range from 10 per cent to 25 per cent of pay. Yet many employees still do not appreciate just how much this benefit is worth. Paternalistic motives are only part of the equation when it comes to an employer deciding on such an expensive commitment. Recruitment and retention are much bigger motivators. Employers will only maximise the value of their investment in pensions by at the same time maximising the value perceived by the workforce – and the workforce cannot value something it does not understand.

So, do employees understand pensions? Apart from those whose employers make a significant effort to get the message across, the evidence points to a resounding 'no'. Had employees understood pensions, we would not have seen so many opting out of occupational schemes and into personal pensions that provided much worse value.

The rest of this chapter concentrates on getting information over effectively to employees so that any misgivings are allayed and, critically, the perceived value of the arrangement can be maximised, thereby maximising at the same time the benefit that an employer gets from this major investment.

Where do we start?

As with most forms of communication, a number of different media exist.

The message may be put across by using any or all of the following:

- brochures and booklets
- presentations
- surgeries
- local pensions officers
- intranet.

Brochures and booklets

A members' booklet is invariably produced for pension schemes. Much of the information that the law requires will be included. Yet many booklets are dry and dull. A few are barely comprehensible. To get the message over, a booklet needs to be:

- written in plain English
- in a sensible format, with an index and a glossary
- well designed
- up to date, in terms of both style and content.

Whilst booklets can be drafted by pensions communication specialists, the job is often left with benefit consultants whose role tends towards the provision of technical support and advice to pensions managers and financial directors. The consultants' 'normal' audience can be very different, in terms of their pensions and financial knowledge, from the average member on the shop floor. It is a good idea, then, to have a draft booklet vetted by a few members, just to see if it makes sense. An annual trustee report also offers a great opportunity to get the message across. If a positive attitude is adopted, and a little time and money spent, the difference in impact can be enormous. So glossy, punchy and positive are the watchwords.

Presentations

Presentations can be very effective but, once again, preparation and planning are critical to success. An effective presentation will have been tailored specifically to the audience. If it has been lifted 'off the shelf', the audience will sense that and may switch off. Presentations are often successful where local and technical knowledge are combined. If it suits the occasion and the subject matter, it can work very well if a local HR person does a presentation jointly with an external pensions consultant.

Employers with significant levels of employee turnover often find this medium very effective, attracting new members using titles such as 'Why You Should Join the Pension Scheme' or the more punchy 'Pensions? What's in it for you?'

Surgeries

Surgeries give employees the opportunity to ask those questions that they may feel uncomfortable airing in a public forum. Employees sometimes feel that they are the only ones who just do not follow how it all works. Others may want to ask about additional voluntary contributions but not let their peers know they have spare cash or their boss know that they hope to fund an early retirement. Trust is crucial, of course, since a desire for confidentiality can often be the main driver. Choosing the right people can be tricky. Employers with large pension schemes and in-house pensions administration departments often appoint a full-time communications person. Employers unable to divert full-time resources to pensions can use their external consultants. This should work well (consultancies are unlikely to send poor communicators) provided trust can be built up quickly.

Pensions helpline

This will fulfil a role similar to that of the surgery, except that access can be remote. For detailed queries, helplines cannot match the face-to-face aspect of surgeries but for run-of-the-mill technical enquiries they can be highly effective.

The employer with the in-house pensions administration function will probably prefer to run its own helpline, while others who outsource their scheme administration should look to their consultants.

Benefit statements

Much of the content of a benefit statement is defined by legislation. This does not excuse bad layout, nor does the information provided need to be restricted to the bare minimum.

A few companies like to produce a *combined* benefit statement. This shows the value of total remuneration paid during the year and could cover basic salary, bonus, pension, car and lunch allowance. For employees, such a statement brings into high relief just how much their employment is worth to them.

Local pensions officers (LPOs)

Employees who spend part of their time acting as local pensions specialists can make the communication process that much more effective. Local pensions officers are likely to be used mainly by those companies with an in-house pensions function. LPOs do not themselves need to be pensions specialists but they do need two key things: training and an interest in the subject.

LPOs should ideally be volunteers, bringing an enthusiasm that press-ganged individuals might lack.

Intranet

More and more companies now use their intranet for their internal communications. Like other HR matters, pensions can use this new medium to good effect.

But the intranet offers something you cannot get from paper communication: interactivity. With an effective and comprehensive site, members can look up 'electronic booklets' but, more than that, they can post questions or participate in discussion forums. More advanced sites can be set up that allow members to check on the status of their benefits and even to have numerical answers provided to questions like 'How much do I need to contribute to retire at 60 with a maximum pension?'

Best practice is for all web pages to be dated and an archive kept of all previous versions.

Have we succeeded?

There are ways to measure whether or not a communication package is working. You can measure the number of questions posed, number of hits on a site, take-up rates in the pension scheme etc. These may be effective (and the knowledge gleaned will probably be very useful) but they should be supported by a more active approach.

The best way to find out what employees think of your new, improved approach to communications is to ask them.

Use surveys either on paper or via the intranet. Let these be confidential, if necessary.

Once you have the results of such surveys, publish them. Then demonstrate, through action, that any feedback has been taken on board.

Pensions cost employers a lot of money. That money is well spent only if the benefits are communicated effectively to employees. And communication is a journey, not a destination.

How do we manage change?

Pensions strategies, by their very nature, are long-term. Any decision to introduce change should not be taken lightly. Well-thought-out pension benefit programmes are aligned with the longer-term business objectives of the employer, the labour market within which the employer competes, as well as being directly or indirectly influenced by legislation.

There are a number of situations that might arise that prompt a review of strategy and ultimately result in a change in the delivery of pension benefits. Common drivers for change are:

- mergers of pension schemes
- cost-containment and cost-saving exercises
- legislative changes
- benefit harmonisation exercises

- employer mergers and acquisitions
- outsourcing of services and associated transfers of employment
- strategic moves from final salary pension provision to money purchase.

Managing change can be a delicate exercise, especially because of the complexity of pensions. Also, employees' appreciation of the importance of pension provision can result in resistance to change. Whilst managing a change in pension provision can be a time-consuming and indeed a daunting task, it does provide the employer with an opportunity to improve the understanding of the basis of pension provision and reinforce the importance and value of the employer's arrangements.

As part of the initial planning for change, the employer must review the fundamental constraints that might exist. Important areas to be investigated include:

- any contractual rights to pension arrangements, whether explicit – in the contract of employment – or inferred from other documents or the way the employer has acted (and which may well require legal advice to identify)
- agreements with trade unions or other employee representative groups covering pension benefits
- previous policy statements
- in occupational schemes, the employer's powers under the trust deed and rules
- legislation.

It is important that the finance and HR functions of the employer work together in establishing the strategy for change – it is unusual for change not to have an impact, whether positive or negative, from both a financial and employee relations perspective.

Planning for the introduction of change

Once the new pension structure has been determined, managing change is fundamentally a communication exercise. It is therefore important that the key messages to be delivered are clearly agreed before the actual drafting of the communication programme starts.

As part of the initial planning phase, a detailed project plan/timetable provides a crucial framework within which the programme of change is to be delivered.

One important early decision that needs to be made is the degree to which there will be employee consultation. This is likely to be determined by the existing lines of communication, if any, between employee representative groups and management, and also the degree to which there is scope for the employer's plans to be modified by the results of any consultation exercise. In addition, there may be agreements with unions or other employee representative groups for any changes to the pay or benefit structures to be first discussed with, or agreed by, that group.

It is important that the communication of change is honest and open and will stand up to scrutiny.

Communicating change

Chapter 8 has already examined ways in which pension arrangements can be communicated. Communicating change will use similar methods. However, the emphasis is most likely to be on statements to individual members, employee presentations and perhaps workshops.

Where feasible, statements showing the effect on members' own personal data can be a powerful tool in answering the inevitable 'what does it mean for me' question. This can, however, be a complex and expensive project – and one that will almost certainly flush out any lurking anomalies.

A written communication is a prerequisite, as it is a permanent record of the change being introduced. It is, however, generally accepted that face-to-face employee presentations, with question-and-answer sessions, produce a dramatic improvement in the success of change programmes. As the presentation programme is rolled out, the same questions will recur. In these circumstances, it is useful to publish a 'Frequently Asked Questions' sheet to ensure that a consistent message is delivered.

In the period after the initial communication of change, it is important that employees have access to further information and the opportunity to obtain answers to remaining questions. Special telephone helplines or e-mail addresses can be useful facilities. Seeking feedback from employee groups on how the change is being received and interpreted means that incorrect rumours can be stopped and, where necessary, improvements made to the communication process.

Change within an existing scheme

When dealing with a change in an occupational pension scheme governed by a trust deed and rules, the power of the employer and trustees to implement change needs to be properly understood. This may result in both parties needing to take legal advice on their powers, duties and obligations under the formal scheme documents.

Often what might be considered routine changes (such as a change to the definition of pensionable salary or life cover benefit) will be instigated by the employer. Trustees will need to consider if benefits already accrued by members are affected in any way by the rule change – if they are, the Pensions Act 1995 places an obligation on trustees to obtain what is known as a section 67 certificate from the scheme actuary to confirm that the value of those accrued benefits is not adversely affected. Where the actuary is unable to provide that certificate, members' individual consent is needed for the changes to go ahead.

Some scheme changes may give rise to a legal obligation on the trustees to disclose information. Similarly, some changes, notably to contracting-out arrangements, require formal notices from the employer.

Moving from final salary to money purchase

As identified in Chapter 4, there is a trend for employers to change benefit basis from final salary to money purchase. Many employers introduce such a change for new employees only and in this context the communication issues are very much the same as introducing a new scheme rather than implementing change.

Smaller employers may typically look to manage such a change for current as well as future employees – in these circumstances the communication will become much more complex. Often, employee groups will perceive the well-known advantages of final salary (eg certainty of benefits) and will recognise the headline disadvantages of money purchase; the communication programme needs to high-light the upsides of the money purchase approach, in terms of the flexibility it introduces and of a more direct sense of 'ownership' of a pot of money, to bring some balance.

For many employees, the money purchase basis is likely to be a new concept with new terminology that needs to be explained. Members will also need to appreciate that there is no longer a guarantee of the benefits payable on retire-ment and that they will need to take a greater interest in investment issues. Often, a new money purchase scheme will contain few investment options but will have a clear default option. Over time, as employee understanding and knowledge builds up, wider investment options can be introduced.

It is important that neither the employer nor the trustees give members financial advice on any decisions they need to make – at least above a purely generic level. Instead, they can be given instructions on how to contact independent financial advisers who will be able to give them detailed individual guidance.

Takeovers and mergers

When corporate transactions result in two or more compa-nies being integrated, the fundamental issue is that ben-efits do not get left to the last minute – it is important to have a seamless changeover to ensure that, for example, life cover benefits are provided at all times. Often the initial confidential discussion in the run-up to a major corporate transaction concentrates on financial and business strategy issues, and benefits and pensions do not feature at all.

As the deal develops, the agreements reached in relation to pensions will be reflected in a pensions schedule to the sale and purchase agreement. The two key issues that the pensions schedule covers are:

- what happens to pensions for transferring employees
- how any surplus or deficit in a transferring pension scheme will be reflected in the price paid.

A common short-term approach for the period immediately following the completion of a transaction is to agree a temporary participation period of up to 12 months during which transferring employees will remain members of their previous employer's pension scheme. The pensions schedule will deal with how the costs of continued membership will be met by the new employer. The agreement of the Inland Revenue will be required for the participation period. The new employer will need to become formally a participating employer in the transferring employer's pension scheme and, if appropriate, an application for a contracting-out certificate will need to be made.

During the temporary participation period, the new employer will need to determine how it will provide future pension benefits for its new employees. The employer may continue with the existing pension structure by setting up a mirror image of the previous scheme (either as a new scheme or as a subsection of an existing scheme), which the transferring employees will be invited to join.

Alternatively, the new employees might be integrated into the existing pension programme of their new employer. This is a more complex issue, depending on whether it results in an improvement or diminution of the value of benefits.

The pensions schedule to the sale and purchase agreement will normally reflect the parties' intentions regarding benefits that have accrued prior to the transaction. It is important to note that the transfer occurs between pension schemes and not employers. Whilst the two employers will be involved significantly in determining strategy, it is, in an occupational scheme environment, a transaction between two groups of trustees.

If both the previous and the new arrangements are money purchase then – subject to there being no early surrender penalties on the transfer of assets – transfers generally occur with little complication. If there is a difference in the investment basis or options (as there almost invariably is), this will need to be explained to members and the appropriate information given to allow them to make informed decisions about the investment of their pension accounts.

If, however, final salary benefits are involved, the issues can become significantly more complicated. Unless the replacement arrangement is a mirror image of the previous arrangement, transfers of accrued benefits will not normally occur at face value on a 'one for one' basis. If benefits come from a less generous to a more generous arrangement, then, for example, only eight months' pensionable service might be credited in the new scheme for each year's service transferred from the previous scheme. Members will need a personal statement confirming their option to transfer – they should be encouraged to take independent financial advice before making their decision.

There are strict legal requirements on which benefit transfers require individual members' consent and those that do not, and on how those transfers must take place.

Transfers of undertakings – TUPE

When a business or undertaking, or part of one, is transferred to a new employer, employees' terms and conditions are for the most part preserved (under the Transfer of Undertakings (Protection of Employment) Regulations 1981, commonly referred to as TUPE). Occupational pension rights, however, are excluded from the protection of TUPE and consequently there is not generally considered to be a legal requirement for the new employer to offer a mirror image scheme. (Group personal pensions, if they are a contractual right of the employee, do not enjoy this exemption. Hitherto, it has been normal practice to set up group personal pensions so as to specifically avoid creating a contractual right. However, this is not possible for new arrangements from 8 October 2001 if the employer is seeking to rely on the arrangement to provide exemption from the stakeholder access requirement – see Chapter 7.)

Despite the TUPE exemption, many employers whose employees are being transferred have, as part of the sale and purchase agreement or other legal document, placed an obligation on the new employer to continue with a mirror image of the benefits in force prior to the transfer. This has particular application in the public sector where companies tendering to supply services are required to provide continued pension rights to transferring employees on a basis 'at least equivalent' to those they enjoyed before. The approach has two key objectives:

- to ensure that profitability is not improved by a reduction in the benefits offered to transferred employees
- to protect the previous employer from claims of constructive dismissal as a result of the terms of the pension transfer.

When tendering for contracts from the public sector, the bidding employer is required to obtain approval from the Government Actuary's Department (GAD) – this is so-called 'passport' approval. GAD will assess the terms of the pension benefits being offered to certify that they consider them to be of similar value. Whilst there is no requirement to provide identical benefits, it is nonetheless generally accepted that a money purchase approach will not receive 'passport' approval if it is replacing a final salary arrangement. (With local authority 'Best Value' contracts, contractors may be able to bypass the 'passport' system by participating in the local authority scheme, at the discretion of the local authority.)

The Government is in the throes of revising the TUPE regulations and a tightening of the requirements for pension provision has been a prominent and controversial subject of consultation.

Further information

Many of the most important sources of information are documents produced by the regulatory bodies.

Opra's *Pension Scheme Trustees* is essential reading for anyone taking on a trustee role. Opra also publishes a range of more specialised guides aimed at both employers and trustees. These are available free from Opra's website (www.opra.co.uk) or in hard copy (Tel: 01273 627600).

The Inland Revenue publishes its *Practice Notes on the Approval of Occupational Pension Schemes (IR12)*, setting out the conditions a scheme must meet in order to gain tax approval. These requirements cover benefits, contributions and certain ongoing administrative duties. The Practice Notes are backed up by periodic Pensions Updates. Again, these documents are available on the Internet (www.inlandrevenue.gov.uk/pensionschemes/) but can also be obtained in hard copy by subscription (Tel: 01268 822855).

As a detailed overview, *Tolley's Pensions Law Handbook* (Butterworths, 2000) is a useful guide. Most benefit consultants and larger law firms issue free news bulletins to those on their mailing lists, to which they will happily add employers and trustees; much information is also available on their websites.

Chartered Institute of Personnel and Development

Customer Satisfaction Survey

We would be grateful if you could spend a few minutes answering these questions and return the postcard to CIPD. <u>Please use a black pen to answer</u>. **If you would like to receive a free CIPD pen, please include your name and address.** IPD MEMBER Y/N

....

1. Title of book ....

2. Date of purchase: month .... year ....

3. How did you acquire this book?
☐Bookshop   ☐Mail order   ☐Exhibition ☐Gift   ☐Bought from Author

4. If ordered by mail, how long did it take to arrive:
☐1 week   ☐2 weeks   ☐more than 2 weeks

5. Name of shop .... Town.. Country ....

6. Please grade the following according to their influence on your purchasing
   decision with 1 as least influential: (please tick)

	1	2	3	4	5
Title					
Publisher					
Author					
Price					
Subject					
Cover					

7. On a scale of 1 to 5 (with 1 as poor & 5 as excellent) please give your impressions
   of the book in terms of: (please tick)

	1	2	3	4	5
Cover design					
Paper/print quality					
Good value for money					
General level of service					

8. Did you find the book:
   Covers the subject in sufficient depth   ☐Yes   ☐No
   Useful for your work   ☐Yes   ☐No

9. Are you using this book to help:
☐In your work ☐Personal study   ☐Both   ☐Other (please state)

Please complete if you are using this as part of a course

10. Name of academic institution..

11. Name of course you are following? ....

12. Did you find this book relevant to the syllabus? ☐Yes ☐No ☐Don't know

Thank you!

To receive regular information about CIPD books and resources call 020 8263 3387.

1795/05/00

Publishing Department

Chartered Institute of Personnel and Development

CIPD House

Camp Road

Wimbledon

London

SW19 4BR